St. Francis
and the Animals Who Loved Him

James F. Twyman

NY Times Bestselling Author

Illustrated by Mauro Lirussi

How to Read
St. Francis and the Animals Who Loved Him

This is a new kind of book. It's not only meant for reading but for listening and singing as well. Each story is accompanied by a song and music video. Whether you're reading this on your own or out loud to a young person, at the end of each story please visit the following website:

www.StFrancisandtheAnimals.com

Let the story come to life with music.

ISBN 9780578826394 (Hardback)
ISBN 9780578818542 (eBook)

Illustrations by Mauro Lirussi

St. Francis
and the Animals Who Loved Him

by James F. Twyman

Illustrated by Mauro Lirussi

Who Was St. Francis of Assisi?

Perhaps you've seen garden statues of St. Francis feeding the birds or paintings of him taming wild wolves. He may have lived eight hundred years ago, but stories about St. Francis and the animals who loved him stir the imagination even today.

Everyone called him Francis or the "Little Frenchman" because his father was conducting business in France when he was born. For the first twenty-four years of his life Francis lived like a prince. He wanted to be like the French troubadours or even a glorious knight riding off to war. His father hoped Francis would bring glory to the family, but instead he was captured during the first battle with neighboring Perugia and was thrown into prison for a year.

By the time he was released Francis was a different person. Fancy clothes and earthly riches were no longer important to him. All he wanted was to praise God through the creatures of God. He would sit in the fields around his home looking at the colorful flowers and watching the wings of the butterflies as they flew overhead. This was his new life.

People have always loved St. Francis, but so did the animals and birds that came to him without fear. These are the stories of the creatures who considered the little friar from Assisi a member of their family.

St. Francis Preaches to the Birds

"Love is flowing from my heart so fast I can't keep it inside. I must find a way to let it out."

Francis said these words as he skipped down a path with several of his friar brothers. They were walking to Bevagna in the Spoleto Valley where hundreds of people were waiting to hear Francis preach, but the other friars knew he wouldn't be able to contain himself much longer.

"If there was a house or a village nearby you could share the Good News with them," Friar Leo said, "but we haven't seen anyone for hours. I'm sure we'll arrive in Bevagna soon."

"I can't wait that long," Francis said as he jumped up and spun in the air. "God is too wonderful and I have to find someone to share this wonderfulness with right now."

"You can share it with us," Friar Bernardo said. "Sing one of the troubadour songs you love so much, but instead of a beautiful maiden we'll imagine our Blessed Lord, or maybe we'll think of his dear mother Mary."

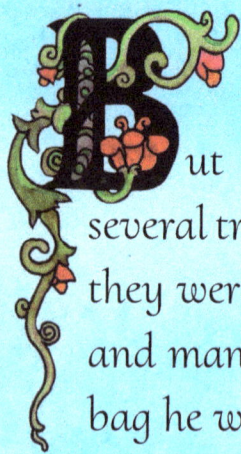

But Francis heard nothing they were saying. His eyes lit on several trees in the middle of a large field a short distance from where they were walking. Hundreds of birds were flying through the sky and many were perched high in the branches. Francis dropped the bag he was carrying and ran as fast as he could in their direction.

"Where are you going, Francis?" Friar Leo called.

"I'm going to preach to the birds," he said. "If there are no people to be found then I'll have to sing to the creatures of God."

The friars ran behind Francis until they all arrived at the group of trees, and the sound of their approach caused many of the birds to spread their wings and fly away.

"No, wait," Francis called to them. "I have something I want to share with you. Hold still and rest awhile and I will tell you about the glorious love that gave you your wings and taught you how to soar through the air. The sky will wait for you if you listen to my words, and when I'm finished you'll fly higher than any bird has ever flown."

As if understanding the words Francis spoke, the birds came to rest on the branches and the ones that had been flying settled at their side. They looked down at the strange little man who spoke as if they shared his language. They tilted their heads in one direction then the next, absorbing the words Francis spoke with their whole being.

"My brother and sister birds, you should greatly praise your Creator and love God with all your energy. He clothed you with feathers and gave you wings for flying. Among all his creatures, God made you free and gave you the purity of air. You neither sow nor reap, but God provides for your every need. He gives you water when you're thirsty and seeds when you're hungry. When Brother Sun disappears below the horizon you rest high in the branches of this tree while Sister Moon reflects his light. And when Brother Sun appears again in the morning you sing and fly about rejoicing in God's love. Yes, you do well to honor your Beloved Lord because of these gifts, and many more which you do not see. But there are many things, I'm sure, that your gentle eyes behold which I am blind to, and for all these things I rejoice. Let your bird-song fill the sky and lift you high into the air. Though I am rooted here on the earth, my soul flies along with you."

s Francis talked the birds seemed to understand every word he spoke. They stretched their necks, spread their wings and opened their beaks. They did not leave that place until Francis finally made the sign of the cross, giving them permission to fly. Then they lifted into the air like a great cloud and the brothers that were with him watched in amazement. Francis then turned back to them.

"Now we can continue walking, my brothers. Now that these wonderful creatures have heard God's message we can preach to the people of Bevagna."

St. Francis Saves Brother Rabbit

One day Francis and two of the friars were on their way to the Eremo Di Montecasale above Sansepolcro when Leo heard a whimpering sound coming from the left side of the path. He jumped into the brush and quickly discovered the source of the sound - a small rabbit caught in a snare. When Francis saw the rabbit he felt a great wave of compassion rise within him.

"Friar Leo," Francis said in a quiet voice, "free the poor creature from the trap as carefully as you can. We don't want to scare it more than it already is."

The rabbit thrashed about as Leo approached, sure these were the men who set the snare. When Leo was finally able to secure the creature he felt the rabbit's heart racing inside its chest. He untied the snare then showed it to Francis and Masseo.

"Bring the creature of God to me so I may console and soothe its spirit," Francis said to him.

Leo laid the rabbit in Francis's hands and within seconds the animal relaxed and lay perfectly still. Leo and Masseo watched this with great wonder and surprise.

"Dear Brother Rabbit," Francis said to his new friend. "You must be careful not to get caught again since we may not be near enough to release you from the trap. You were made to praise God with your happy, carefree life. But there are many in this forest who would rather see you as a meal on their table than a holy creature created by a holy God. Go now and find your family. I'm sure they are terribly worried about you."

Francis kissed the rabbit on its soft head then set it down as tenderly as he could. The rabbit looked up at Francis, who was sitting on the ground, as if wondering what he should do next. To everyone's surprise he did not run into the forest as they thought, but jumped back into Francis's lap and rested there, perfectly content.

Francis picked the rabbit up and looked straight into its watery eyes.

"My dear brother rabbit, you cannot stay with us. We're on our way to visit our brothers at the hermitage and it won't do to show up with you in my hands. The friar cook might think we brought a meal to share with the brothers and since I cannot watch over you every second it would be better for you to go and find your family. Run away now and give glory to God for your life."

Once again Francis set the rabbit down on the ground but it jumped back into his lap.

"This creature thinks it found a home in your soft habit," Friar Masseo said to Francis. "Give him to me and I'll take him deep into the forest and set it free. But you and Friar Leo should start walking since the rabbit will likely follow me hoping to rest in your lap again."

Francis thought this was a good idea and picked the rabbit up, blessing it before giving it to Friar Masseo.

"God is the only protection you need," Francis said to the rabbit. "I'm honored you want to stay with us, but it would be better to follow Masseo's advice."

Francis and Leo watched Masseo and Brother Rabbit as they disappeared into the forest, but as they went the rabbit took a final look back at the saint.

Their hearts would always be connected though they would never see each other again.

The Fish That Loved St. Francis

Francis and Friar Leo were on their way to visit the brothers living in Greccio but it was already late in the afternoon and a huge lake lay between them and the friary. Leo suggested they walk around the lake but Francis had a different idea.

"Our Blessed Lord will provide another way," Francis said calmly. "If we try walking all the way around we won't arrive until morning and the brothers have prepared a simple feast for our arrival."

Just then a tall man came out of the forest holding a long oar and almost ran into the two friars as he walked to the edge of the lake.

"Mamma mia," the man exclaimed. "You should make a noise when another man approaches so he doesn't run into you." Then he looked at Francis and a smile lit across his face. "Wait, you're him, Francis from Assisi. I heard you preach once in Poggio Bustone.

My wife and I are both hoping to become members of your third order one day. Why are you standing here looking out over the lake so late in the day?"

"Yes, it is very late and we're expected at our friary in Greccio," Francis said to the man. "Am I correct in believing that you have a boat nearby? If so, then we would be eternally happy for a lift to the other side of the lake."

"Yes, I do have a boat, just inside those bushes there," the man said, "and it would be a great honor to take both of you to the other side. You may call me Antonio the boatman. I am at your service, dear friars."

ith that the men pulled the boat from the bushes and dragged it to the lake, then climbed inside. Antonio stayed to the rear of the boat and Leo was in the front, leaving Francis in the center. A light wind came up from behind and it didn't take more than thirty minutes for them to arrive on the other side. Antonio jumped into the water and pulled the boat ashore.

"Look who I found," he said to a group of fishermen who stood nearby. "It's the great saint of Assisi, Friar Francis and Friar Leo. Now my boat has been blessed and tomorrow it will surely catch the heaviest load of fish."

The men clamored to have a look and were amazed to see such a famous man grace their tiny village.

"You must stay with us awhile," one of them said to Francis. "Look, here is a fish I caught a few moments ago. It would be my honor to have you and your brother stay and eat with us tonight."

The man placed the fish, which was still very much alive, into Francis's hands. It flipped back and forth trying to escape, and Francis held it up to his eyes and looked deep into its soul.

"I could never eat such a wonderful creature," he said to the men. "Look into his eyes and you'll see God's love shining forth. If it would not offend you, I would like to return it to the lake so it may live and praise our Lord. Please, brothers, give me this one small favor."

The men looked each other and all of them agreed.

"It was a gift and you can do anything you like with it," the man who gave him the fish said.

Francis stroked the head of the fish one last time, then returned it to its home. They expected it to swim away as soon as it had a chance, but it remained there looking up at Francis. Leo noticed this, then tossed a small stone into the water hoping it would force the fish to swim toward deeper water. But it did not move, swimming just beneath the surface of the water looking up at the man who showed it so much mercy.

"I think the fish is in love with you," Antonio said. But the man who gifted the fish to Francis disagreed.

"Stop speaking like that, Antonio. Fish like this one are incapable of love."

"It's not true," Francis said as he turned around. "Everything created by God is capable of love, no matter how different they may seem, because every created thing reflects the source of all love. Even sister fish who swims before us now responds to a simple act of kindness. She knows she was meant for the skillet and yet here she is swimming and praising the Lord. So, who's to say a fish like this one can't fall in love, even if it's with a creature as unworthy as me?"

They looked again at the fish which continued to look up at Francis, and everyone present had the feeling they were witnessing a miracle. Francis finally knelt down at the bank of the lake and spoke directly to his new friend. He made the sign of the cross in the air and said:

"It's time for you to go back to your family, sister fish. I bless you and wish you a long life and a happy end. Go now, and spread the good news you've heard today with the entire world beneath the surface of this lake."

As soon as he finished the fish flapped its tail and disappeared from their sight. Francis stood up and turned toward the crowd which had grown to be over a hundred people.

"And now it's time for us to leave you. Our brothers in Greccio are waiting with a fresh loaf of bread and rich olive oil. It will be a simple meal, but nothing more is required for those so full of God's love."

Francis and Leo walked away toward the friary, and the entire crowd stood there watching them until they finally disappeared over the hill.

St. Francis Saves Sister Spot

One day St. Francis was walking toward the Porta Nuova, the gate that leads into Assisi, when he heard a great commotion on the other side.

When he passed through the gate he saw a group of young boys terrorizing a small dog with a single black spot on its back. The poor creature cowered in the corner while the boys threw mud and small stones at it, unable to escape. Francis ran at the boys yelling for them to leave.

They scattered and left Francis alone with the dog.

The small dog hid its face from Francis as if it was ashamed but the saint slowly walked up to it and offered his hand in a sign of friendship.

"Have no fear, Sister Cagna (dog). The boys are gone and will harm you no more. My name is Brother Francis and I love all of God's creatures, especially ones that are friendless and alone, like you."

Sister Cagne took a tentative step toward Francis then sniffed his hand. She could sense his compassion and gave his hand a lick.

"That's better, dear sister," Francis said to her. "I know what it feels like to be ridiculed and have people throw rocks and mud at me. It wasn't very long ago, when I first surrendered my fancy clothes and inheritance, that boys followed me around Assisi making fun and calling me terrible names. They said I was a fool because I chose richness over riches and goodness over goods. My only desire was to know and love God, and that threatened the people who said such things with their mouths but not with their hearts."

The dog climbed up into Francis's lap and rested her head on his leg.

"But there's a secret I learned, Sister Cagna, a secret I've never mentioned to anyone else before now. It's a secret that changed my life completely, and I believe it could change the entire world if people would embrace it with their hearts. Would you like to hear the secret I learned, sister?"

Sister Cagna looked up at him as if saying she did want to hear. Francis lightly touched the spot on the dog's back and said:

"There is no spot where God is not. That's it. God is everywhere and is hidden nowhere. We may close our eyes and refuse to see, but that doesn't mean God is absent. And look at you. God has given you a great gift by putting this spot on your back. It's here to remind you of the secret I learned, and for others to learn it through you.

Whenever you pass a mirror and see the spot on your back I want you to remember how blessed you. And I will do the same, dearest sister."

It was as if the little dog understood each words Francis spoke. It wagged its tail with happy enthusiasm.

"We all have spots we want to hide, as if they make us less lovable, but the opposite is true. I love you because of your spot, and I love everyone in the same way. Most of all, I love myself in spite of the many spots that cover my soul because of poor decisions I've made, and I know that God loves me, and you, and everyone even more. And that's why we must praise God above everything of this world, because he loved us so much he gave us his own beloved son."

Francis pulled the dog closer and gave it a hug, then set it back down on the ground.

"One final thing, Sister Cagna. The secret I told you isn't a secret at all. I'm going to tell everyone I meet, and I want you to do the same. I know that you don't have the gift of words, but you can look upon everyone you meet with love, including the boys who were so unkind to you. You can bless them with your eyes and remind them how much God loves them. Now go and praise the Lord, and remember - there is no spot where God is not!"

The little dog turned and walked down the street and Francis watched it go. His heart was filled with love for he knew that Sister Cagna now had a ministry to fulfill, sharing the secret that's really no secret at all.

Brother Falcon Helps St. Francis

St. Francis loved to be alone in the mountains where he could pray and feel God's presence. His favorite retreat was a tiny cave near the top of Mount Subasio, a forty-five minute walk above Assisi, but there was another cave on a mountain in Tuscany that was just as peaceful - La Verna.

Brother Leo often accompanied Francis on the long journey and when they finally arrived the two exhausted friars walked to their hermitage caves for a rest.

"My feet are sore and my back aches, Brother Leo. I long for the silence of my cave where I can hear God's voice clearly."

Brother Leo nodded and smiled.

"I will not delay your rest, Brother Francis. Go to your cave and if you need anything I will be there to serve you."

Francis hiked to his cave and lay his head on the rock that served as a pillow. He was almost asleep when he heard a loud screeching noise coming from a tree outside the cave. It pierced his ears and made him jump. Francis stood up and walked outside, then looked up into the trees. He saw a huge falcon looking down at him with fiery eyes.

"**B**rother Falcon, I know this is your home and I am just a visitor, but I implore you to let me sleep awhile. It took us eight long days to walk from Assisi and I need to rest before vespers."

The huge bird opened its beak and screeched even louder. Francis realized that he wasn't going to convince the falcon so he decided to try a different approach. He knelt down and began singing a chant he wrote on the way to La Verna. If the bird was going to sing so loud, then he would do the same.

"Oh Lord, all glorious, all merciful and good, I lift my heart to thee. Great God, so perfect, if only you could let Brother Sun shine down upon me."

The falcon stopped screeching and looked down at the small friar as if curious and amused. And it did not make another sound.

"I thank you, Brother Falcon. I pray that you give me just one hour of rest, then you can sing all you want."

The bird shook its wings as if agreeing to the terms, then climbed higher into the tree to give Francis the privacy he needed.

Exactly one hour later Francis awoke to the Falcon screeching outside the entrance of the cave. Francis stood up and bird flew into the tree just above Francis's head.

"I asked for an hour and it looks like you gave me exactly that. I thank you, Brother Falcon. And now it's time for me to pray."

It was St. Francis's custom to rise minutes before the first rays of sunlight touched the earth so he could praise God before it was time for morning prayer. But the journey from Assisi had taken its toll, and Francis did not wake up as he usually would. A minute or two later Brother Falcon opened his beak and let out a loud cry. The sound startled Francis and he opened his eyes, then sat up.

"You have done me a great favor, dear brother. I might have slept right through the time for prayer if not for you."

The falcon looked pleased and flew higher into the tree while Francis knelt down in his cave to begin his prayers.

Happy to have such an important job, that of waking a saint for morning prayer, Brother Falcon returned each morning to welcome Francis to a new day. And every time he did, Francis thanked him and blessed him before the great bird flew off.

But then one day, everything changed. During the night Francis developed a slight fever and only slept a few hours. When morning came and it was time for prayer, Brother Falcon sensed something was wrong. He looked down at the entrance of the cave and felt the energy of the saint. He realized Francis needed more rest, so he sat on the tree branch without making a sound. Two hours later Francis woke up feeling much better. Then he looked up into the tree and saw his friend.

"Dear brother, you didn't wake me with your happy noise this morning. Did you know that I was ill and needed more rest?"

Brother Falcone stretched out his mighty wings and Francis realized he understood his words. Then the great bird let out a loud cry that made Francis laugh.

"Thank you, Brother Falcon. You are better than the bells of Assisi."

St. Francis Tames Brother Wolf

St. Francis heard about the wolf of Gubbio when he and Friar Leo were leaving Assisi to begin a long journey. He turned to his companion and said: "This poor creature of God is so misunderstood. I'm not sure if I should go and tame the wolf or the people of Gubbio."

"But Francis," Leo said, "I heard that the wolf is terribly fierce and that several people have been devoured by it. Maybe we should avoid the area altogether."

But Francis was already of his way and Leo had to run to keep up with him. They arrived in Gubbio the next day and when the people saw the poor man from Assisi enter the city gates they were overjoyed.

"You must save us from this terrible animal," an older woman said to him. "The men of this town are so afraid they won't even leave the city walls to defend us."

"And how is that ridiculous looking friar going to help us?" a stout red-faced man said. "Look at him, he's dressed in rags and looks like he couldn't even defend himself against a puppy, let alone a vicious wolf."

rancis ignored the man and turned to the old woman.

"Where might I find this creature so that I may convince it to convert its life?"

"You don't need to look far," she said to him. "His lair is not far from the city gates. He waits there for anyone unwise enough to stray from the town alone."

"Friar Leo, let's make our way there now," Francis said as he turned and began walking to the gate. "We don't have any time to lose."

Leo followed Francis as did around fifty people who heard that the famous friar from Assisi had come to save them, or be eaten by the beast. Either way, they didn't want to miss the scene.

Within minutes of leaving the city they heard a low rumbling sound coming from a rocky area near a forest of trees. The woman pointed in that direction and said: "That is where the wolf lives. Please, Brother Francis, this is a bad idea. I don't think it will end well for you."

But Francis did not hear her and was on his way toward the wolf's lair. Leo and the crowd remained behind and several women fell to their knees in prayer. When the saint traveled a short distance he heard the sound of rustling leaves, then saw the enormous wolf charging at full speed. Francis stood watching the animal and when it came near he made the sign of the cross and said in a loud voice:

"That's far enough, Brother Wolf. In the name of Jesus hold still and listen to me."

The wolf stopped in its tracks as if confused. Its teeth were bared but it came no closer. Francis took two steps forward then sat down on the ground, no more than ten feet from the ferocious animal.

"Brother Wolf, you've done terrible things and have inspired much fear in this land. Men and dogs chase you and seek your life, all because you've chosen the path of anger and aggression. But it doesn't have to continue. I know you're as afraid as the people of Gubbio, and that you began these attacks because of your great hunger. But there is a solution if you're willing to agree. If you change your ways and live in peace I assure you that the people of Gubbio will supply everything you need. They will leave food for you and care for you as a member of one family. If you agree to the condition of peace I promise that this standoff will end."

The wolf tilted his head as if he understood every word Francis spoke. His enormous ears lay against his head and instead of showing his fangs the huge animal began to pant like a dog. Then it slowly walked over to Francis and held out its paw. Francis took it in his hand and the agreement was sealed.

"Then we have an understanding. From this day on you will be considered family and will co-exist with these fine people in peace."

The citizens of Gubbio who watched from a distance were amazed. They thought they had come to see a saint devoured by a wolf but instead the wolf seemed like a tame house pet. From that day forward the agreement was kept and the people of Gubbio treated Brother Wolf as an honored guest in the town.

St. Francis and Sister Pheasant

"Our dear father is nearing the end of his life," Friar Leo told St. Clare as they stood at the door of San Damiano. Clare, who promised to never leave her convent, felt torn and wondered if she should go to the man who inspired her to leave everything and follow Christ. Just then a nobleman from Assisi approached carrying a live pheasant he intended to give to Clare and the other sisters. Clare took the beautiful bird into her arms.

"I shall send this gift to our spiritual father in my absence," Clare said to Leo. "It will bring him great joy."

"But Sister Clare, you know Francis would never kill such a creature of God."

"This pheasant is not for eating but for lifting his spirits." Then she handed it to Leo and darted back into her cloister.

A short while later Leo returned to Our Lady of the Angels where the friars lived and stepped inside the tiny room where Francis lay. He took one look at the beautiful bird and called for Leo to bring it to him. He took it into his arms and caressed it as if it were a tiny child.

"This is a gift from our sister Clare," Leo said to Francis. "She said it would lift your spirits and inspire health."

"It has already done so," Francis said. "Oh, blessed creature of God, how beautiful you are. And though I would love to keep you with me to remind me of my spiritual daughter, you were not meant for this room. You were made for the field and for the sky. Leo, please take Sister Pheasant and release her outside these walls. Only then will this gift please God."

Leo did as he was told and took the bird outside, leaving the door open so Francis could witness the release. He set it down on the ground expecting it to fly away, but instead it ran passed Leo and back into the arms of the saint.

"Dear sister," Francis said, "my gratitude for your love is boundless and the joy you bring is like a balm to my soul. But it would be wrong to keep you here."

ust then a doctor came into the room and saw Sister Pheasant. Leo told him everything and asked for his advice.

"Give me the bird and I will take it to my home," he said. "I promise no harm will come to her and I will let her roam my large property at will."

Francis agreed and with tears in his eyes, watched the doctor take the bird away.

As if terribly sad over the loss of Francis's embrace, the pheasant refused to eat or drink and after three days the doctor decided to bring the bird back to the friary. As soon as the door opened and she saw Francis laying in the bed it flew to him and rested in his arms. After some time he set the bird down and it began to eat the seeds they offered.

"God's gifts are so unexpected," Francis said as he watched.

St. Francis and the Animals Who Loved Him

It was late in the afternoon on October 3, 1226 when St. Clare entered the tiny hut where her spiritual father lay ready to return to God. This was the first time Clare had left her convent at San Damiano in ten years, but she had to see Francis one final time. She arrived and saw him laying on a straw bed, his eyes blind and his breath shallow, but when he felt Clare's presence he sat up and seemed to come back to life.

"My dear Clare," Francis said to her. "Come and sit with me."

Clare sat down on a tiny stool next to the bed and took Francis's hand.

"I am here, beloved friend," she said. "I came as soon as I received word from Friar Leo. You were always there for me and now I am here for you."

"There's something I want you to hear," Francis said to her. "My heart is so full of love for all of God's creatures, I had to express my devotion one final time. I can no longer see through these earthly eyes but my spiritual eyes are open wide, and they can see so far. I dictated a prayer to Friar Alias that I want you to hear it. This is how I want to leave this earth, singing with joy to the creatures that God loves so much."

rancis motioned to Friar Alias to read the prayer he wrote, and everyone in that small room bowed their heads knowing that this was the final testament of their brother and dearest friend. Alias picked up the parchment, took a deep breath and began to read:

Most High, all-powerful and good Lord,
praised be you, with all your holy creatures
especially Brother Sun, through whom you bring us light.
He is beautiful and radiant and bears the likeness of you, Holy One.

And praised be you through Sister Moon and all the stars.
In Heaven you formed them - clear and precious and beautiful.
Praised be you, my Lord, through Brother Wind and Sister Air,
and clouds and every kind of weather.

Praised be you through Sister Water who is very useful and precious and chaste.
Praised be you through Brother Fire through whom you light the night.
He is beautiful and playful and robust and strong.

And praised be you through Sister Mother Earth who sustains us and who produces various fruits and colored flowers and herbs.
Finally, praised be you, my Lord, through Sister Bodily Death from whom no one can escape.
Praise and bless my Lord and give thanks.
Serve him with great humility.

St. Francis lay in his bed smiling as he heard the prayer, and Clare let a single tear fall from her eye. Just then one of the friars opened the door and rushed into the room.

"Sister Clare, you must see this. Come outside and see."

Clare and a few others who were in the room followed the friar outside and looked around with great amazement. Animals were coming out of the forest to honor the man who loved them so well. Birds filled the air and the branches of every tree, including a huge falcon who balanced himself on a branch very near the hut where Francis lay. They saw Brother Rabbit sitting quietly next to a large boulder and a huge wolf came lumbering out of the forest looking tame and loving. Then they saw a beautiful pheasant coming from another direction and many other creatures.

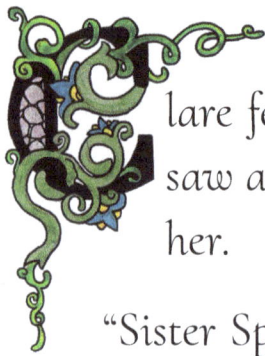

Clare felt something scratch at her leg. She looked down and saw a small dog with a single spot on her back looking up at her.

"Sister Spot," she said as more tears began to flow. "You've come to see him again." She reached down and picked up the dog. "Come with me, dear sister. He will be so happy to see you."

Clare and the others stepped into the hut and Clare walked to the side of the bed.

"Dear brother, I have someone who would like to rest with you for a while," Clare said as she lay Sister Spot in his arms. Francis's face lit up with joy.

"Sister Cagna," he said. "I knew I would see you again. What a precious gift you have given me returning one last time."

"It is not just her," Friar Bernardo said. "Every creature you ever loved has returned to tell you how much they love and admire you. There are birds of every color and shape, rabbits and even the wolf of Gubbio has come. If only you could see them with your eyes."

"But I can see them with my heart," Francis said as he held Sister Spot in his arms. "The love we share will always return to us, for love is the force that binds us together and makes us one."

Later that night, surrounded by the creatures who loved him, Francis closed his eyes and released his soul to God.

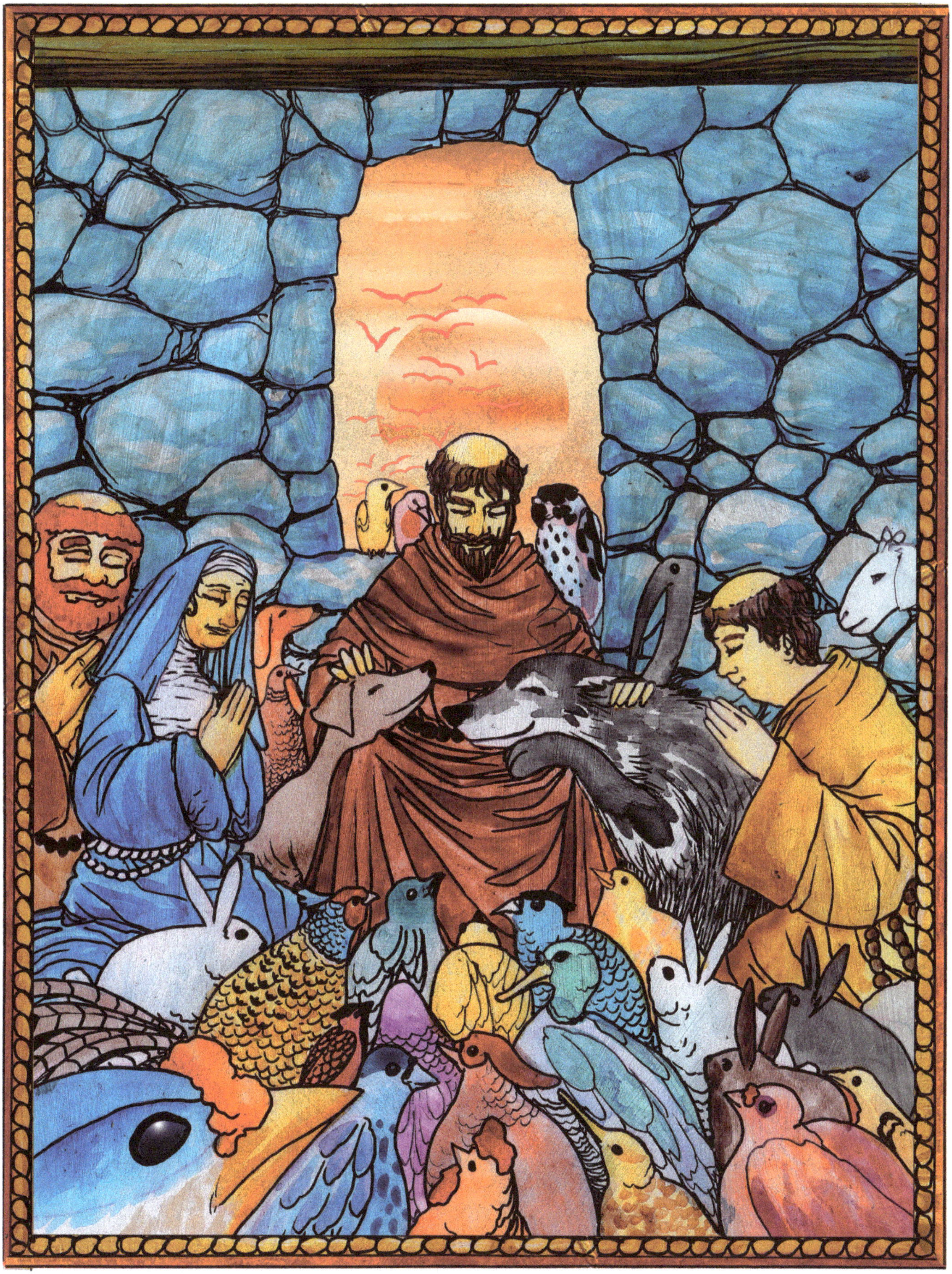

www.ingramcontent.com/pod-product-compliance
Lightning Source LLC
Chambersburg PA
CBHW040302100426
42811CB00011B/1339